Some Days

Some Days

poems by
Garnette Mullis

The University of Arkansas Press
Fayetteville   1994

98   97   96   95   94   5   4   3   2   1

Designed by Gail Carter

The paper used in this publication meets the minimum
requirements of the American National Standard for
Permanence of Paper for Printed Library Materials
Z39.48-1984. ♾

Library of Congress Cataloging-in-Publication Data
Mullis, Garnette.
        Some days : poems / by Garnette Mullis.
            p.   cm.
        ISBN 1-55728-299-4 (c). — ISBN 1-55728-300-1 (p)
        PS3563.U3987S66   1994
        811'.54—dc20   93-32772
                                                CIP

Contents

Some Days

My Mother, the Photographer

The shade, the light were not easily managed.
Despite snags in arranging her children,
my mother planned entire albums of events
to bind us all together in time.
Here, two are seated, two stand,
Here, the girls wear hats, the boys jackets.
Here, my brothers grin, my sister's smile blurs,
My mother's precision
placed us in these clusters.

I remember her waving her arms
until our group satisfied her ideas for a family
then moving the camera from her right hand
to her left until we all held still.

She could not see
that our separate visions met only for a moment
at the dark boundary of her body.
She could not know the way her features,
the texture of her dress
would fade out of the sunlight,
leaving a pose to steady our glances.

There are no photographers among her children,
I search again from snapshot to snapshot
for the shadow she must have cast,
It is nowhere on these pages of photographs.

The Perfect Child

There is one memory:
when we left our yard
for the forbidden corner
then ran across the idle afternoon street.
We walked home to be punished together.

Those days, it was the crossing that surprised us—
the way our twin shadows led us,
one's hand in the other's
across the yard,
the field,
the small town's pavement in summer.

Above

If that was my mother's soul
that hovered like a hummingbird
of light above her corpse
then rose until the funeral home
was roofless, how she
must have sighed to need no breath
after years of the body breathless
and frightened. Still,
when I saw the small ghost
departing, I turned to touch
the cool skin that was left
and lost sight of that final
shiver of spirit—my mother
sustained by nothing at last.

Some Days

Some days, with all of them gone—his wife back
in the city, his daughter at college,
his brother drunk with a mood wet and black—
the background emerged: trimmers cutting hedge,
the maid's slow, faithful hymn dusting downstairs,
and then, for an instant, his thoughts just stopped.

Once, hunting, when mallards flared up the air,
he stared across the reeds where the birds dropped
until his buddies' talk sounded coarse.
Separations, he thought, *happen. They happen.*
But the solitude still held him close,
so he told himself they'd all come home again.
In truth, he felt it wasteful to grow too sad,
a man of his years who had all he had.

Grease

My grandmother used to say
stay away from the windows (in Memphis
where she lived on the eleventh floor
of an old hotel)
because if you fall, you will be a
grease spot
on the street.
This motto was spoken over every windowsill.
I felt I would have liked to be
a grease spot
in Memphis on the street.

A Splintered Railing

Once my father's glance
meant safety
from the circle of doubts
beyond the light of his reading lamp,
and I carried a borrowed certainty
into my dreams.

This morning, near dawn, he stood
beside a splintered railing
over a rough body of water.
At first he watched me,
then he turned away

and my faith in his vision
vanished. Beginning
as simple restlessness,
my body said, *Wake up!*

World Series

The pitcher was Tom Seaver.
Summer nights while my sister slept in the second bed,
my grandmother dozed in the TV light,
small bones piled in a wheelchair.

Awakening, she spoke as if,
following dreams,
she could broadcast to him. "Come on, Tommy," she said.

Last night at a bar thirteen men and I watched
a baseball game,
connected to one another by a screen on the wall.

I was glad to be the woman there,
to have learned from her some
of how the game is played
but, inadequate for it all,
unable to remember her hero of those fragile days.

At home, near sleep, I said his name.
Hers traveled through me. Julie.
I want your mumbled cheers,
my sister in her slumber across the hall.

J Fall

My bed is made, I'll sleep in it.
My mother's mother stitched the quilt
of girls who stand in pantalettes
ruffled beneath their cotton skirts—
a quilt taken back from a lover
who was lanky like my father
and who wanted a memento. Blood
stains the skirt of a girl in blue.

Pillows and sheets of butterflies
are brighter than the quilt but will not keep.
Upon their wide wings I close my eyes.
Between memory and flight, I fall asleep.

Album

for Lynn

In the photograph you have sent me
I see the South with an old brick wall,
laced at the side by a wide gardenia bush.
Three girls in the foreground are posing
in cotton sundresses, ribbons, braided hair.

The tallest one, between the others,
folds her hands backward onto her hips,
squints her demands into the light.
Later, she will be fat.
Here, her slender bones
have begun their defiant reach for size.

The second in height, given to smiling,
turns her face to the camera fully.
Just above her, a flower dangles like a crown.
She could shelter her heart
then tilt her head toward those watching,
bestow a blessing on the photographer.

The smallest child has been observing
and has folded her hands at the space between her legs

to mimic the second, lively girl.
They have formed a triangle of will or love.
Surely they have been playing together

or rehearsing to carefully lift their arms
and begin a figured dance—
the slighter girls circling their grave, central sister—
or preparing to run out of our vision
to a brother's shoulders,
that would frame this scene with laughter.

Should I object that already the requirements
of locale, costume, predicted posing
have taken hold of these young lives?
Give them time you meant to say,
while I watch this moment last for years.

Of Course

for Michelle

If I someway could have changed the long course
of the last six months, I would have had Sam,
your son, born with his full left arm and hand
and I would not have lost my own right breast.
Instead, his right hand forms a small, tight fist
and I say, *Sorry I can't help crying,*
then stop. Death's the thing I think I'm deciding
while the baby mouths and sucks at your breast.
Once we said we'd be friends our whole long lives.
Now, in the slow noise of birth and illness,
it's being through time that soothes and fills us.
My fears dissolve like a dream of knives.
Of course, we decide little in the end;
even love's a gift that buckles and bends.

Card Shop

The Wyoma Card Shop is still
plop in the heart of Lynn.
Barely bigger than my car,
it was painted blue years ago.
Its decorated bells rarely sell.
Its dedicated saleslady
has turned dark with age
and has very little hair.

I pass the Wyoma Card Shop
in a blizzard. Ahead is a cemetery
with corpses as old as the nation
under their independence stones.

New England, fresh and filthy,
let freedom ring.

Aid

This group at shore has unnerved me
with its cautious, lively talk.

Out on the foam, a small white bird
with one curled wing

rocks into each wave,
pointing to deeper water.

If I decided to give my aid,
how would I explain?

If I left the shore to walk
and carry the crippled thing,

mine would become the exact shape
the creature would have to flee.

Conversation

I see them on a noisy horizon
of people and mirrors, their faces turned first
away from, then toward, each other.
She is asking about his sisters.
He is proud of the youngest, brightest one.
He asks about her brothers, saying he met
a man in Tucson who reminded him
of her brothers. He has wanted to call them
to hunt or fish along a southern river.
She says they don't talk to each other now.

He says he still loves a good argument.
She is saying he should call the younger
of her brothers who would be glad to hear.
He says he wants to move to the water.
And children. He wants his children to be
all his. He laughs; a bright shine crosses
his dark eyelashes. He says he has stopped
expecting affection. Then she is able to touch
his arm, as lightly as memory
reshaping alarm. Just the way we see
the moon's reflected light, the cold it casts
over porches and doorways, she begins denying
the brittle, predictable passing
of time—and turns away to smile.

The Guest

Again you think of someone distant.
You look out of the window
of someone else's kitchen
at the two-story house
bordering this back yard
just as the sun is brushing
the pale sleeve of its nightgown
across the dusty windows
of this neighborly town.

Schooled in glad-hearted visitation,
you forget that night draws you
toward any home at all.
You say good night to this group of residents,
carry a glass of water up
these carpeted stairs,
then, touching the lamp switch
and lifting the cat from the bed,
you frown into the mirror and wonder
how you would rearrange the room.

The Imaginary Retreats of Sadness

in memory of Jean Stafford

When I had read *The Mountain Lion*, had learned
how Molly died, my throat ached
as though the bullet that blew
her small head apart could ricochet. Molly,
redheaded lovelessness, victim of fictional
death, I'm practicing now. Now I say,
I won't miss you a bit.

You never knew a thing about me and if you say
you did, I'll make up the meanest lie
you've heard yet and tell loathesome Follansbee
himself. I think it's working, Molly.
Despite this tiny wound, see how, for two
of us, I keep the sadness at bay?

Kayak

How contemporary the kayakers appear to be,
set on the brown fabric of the display
where they add to our modern perspective
the way rough waters once were a threat.
Their expressions are shaded from the light
by striped wooden visors with clear feathers
splaying behind, fit for a temperate beach

in July. The paddler in front, a male,
balances an oar with double blades
in outstretched hands. His companion's hands
rest against the little craft
as if she had laid winning cards
face-down to the inlay of a game table
and paused to consider her luckiest bid.

Both are wearing bird-skin parkas
with gut-skin protectors closely tied
below the shoulders into the canoe.
He leans to the left, handling the boat.
She raises her head, calms her face,
masking the knowledge that fate is fate.
Today water is only the miracle of water.

The Pastry Shop

Beyond carved, vaulted arches, Evensong's last chords
hover at the doors of the cathedral. Its stoneyard
inventory of angels and griffons watches over
sirens and street musicians. Across the way,
the pastry shop fills with an after-church crowd,
the line leaning over the counter, eyeing almonds
and chocolate. An old man in back straightens his paper;
asks again for a glass of water. *Who,* he wonders,
hasn't gone into mother's purse for a quarter?
Above, like a ring of breath on a window, the gibbous moon
stares back at the breathers. Chill fills the newscast:
at the corner, a man has trembled, slipped from the curb
that was prayer bench, stepladder, his point of balance.
Still mumbling, *Now, let's just have a look . . .* , he edges
toward the pastry shop's leaded-glass door, uncertain
of the hunger that's a pale, laced wrapping for his portion
of delicately layered, tart, prayed-over sorrow.

Poem

Sometimes when I'm alone and night approaches
as though night were something special, I begin
to be afraid—the way I used to be afraid
when I awakened from a bad dream and could hear
that everyone in the house had gone to sleep.
That's a difficult time for a child, knowing
that those who should be watching out are not.

Ribs

In midtown Manhattan on Saturday,
it's nearly three o'clock
when I look up
at the high metal ribs
of a facade going up
or coming down,
reflecting light
from another tall building.
True, God with God's vague labels
may not bless or recognize
the City. We may stand
in a dungeon
into which fresh light
has just fallen. But the ribs
of the skywise building are shining,
and the cold air on my face
has lightened the little deaths
that frighten us all. Today
the tall ribs of a building
have turned gold in the sun
and while I ask nothing,
just for a moment everything is given.

Sea Guide

As day comes, a sea gull cries and sails
high in a courtyard of glass and stone.
From ground to sky, sleepers awakened
by the floating vestige of the shore,
lost and longing for that freedom of the sand
to change its morning shape
beneath the water's hand,
turn and sigh—couples woven through habit
together, children kept from one another
by dark's uncertainty, old people waiting
to die in dreams—wake up, disturbed
by the call of a water bird
hovering within the human horizon
and move down to the pavements of April,
cautious of this city, our hand-built miracle.

Jimmy

Jimmy McPherson, could you remember
what it was like naked and thin
under your bed? Or the sharp orange flavor
of the children's aspirin
we swallowed pill by pill? I remember
getting caught by your mother,
your small index finger
stuck in my navel. I remember drowsily
crossing the black-and-white linoleum
in my parent's kitchen
while my mother talked to the pediatrician.
You sneered that I was a sissy whenever I cried.

It went on that way—
the little pleasures in wickedness revoked
until I hated those lessons of trivial danger
and the few words of gossip I heard:
that you grew up huge, often picked fights,
for the past five years
had worked on a river barge crew.

Then I dreamed you hanged yourself
from the checkered ceiling of the bare berth
allotted for the six days it should have taken

to navigate the southern Mississippi
(you were six hours out of Memphis)
on a huge black boat without portholes.

I dreamed I could see your plump face
up close. I counted twenty-three lashes
surrounding each dark blue eye,
then, stepping back to the door,
thought *now he must really be dead!*
Laughing, I turned to the big barge's captain
to say, *Jimmy was always a sissy.*
As a child he was never any fun at all.

Mirror, Mirror

The night the huge mirror broke above
the rattan couch on your mother's porch,
I should have paid attention. It startled me
the way it suddenly dropped off the wall.
Excusing bad luck, I pushed the number
seven away. I had been practically
begging your mother to read your story
(I sometimes feel I begged my own mother
to see the joy that was in my father)
and she had been shaking her head and you
sat across the room, all magic vanished.
I should have paid attention. After all,
you had known each other all of your life.
Who was I to act at understanding?
Now six years have passed since that, our first
May together. At the end, I'm able
to remember it wasn't the mirror
but a shard of its crystal frame that shattered.
No one was hurt, though we all were shaken.

Separation

I must have left home long ago.
My symbols for it are gravestones
echoing in evening with cunning prayers
while the dead readjust their plans.

Sonatina

1.

The notes drop
lower and lower
as though a piano,
violin, any human
tune had solemn reasons.
Once, and young, she
cried to be rid of loss.
Other times,
in memory of that swaying,
she only drew near
an irrevocable moment
with her shadow.

If we were sisters,
she told her friend,
we could end this
alarming laughter.

2.

It is spring
in January and the air
is full of foolish
gravelly light.
The ditch grass talks
of small animals
awakening too soon.
The road she runs on
has become, by accident,
a new horizon
between two separate worlds.
But they are fields
and only fields.
Ducks here. Dogs there.
Cars one way. Cars the other.
Breath, deep air, is all that matters
when the house on the higher line
of the hill begins its watching.

Isaac's Afternoon

Though I have no way of knowing
what parts of the story are true,
I believe Abraham did
lead his son to Moriah.
It's an isolated story.
Isaac would have a different version—
a memory of the wind's speed that day,
of laughter somewhere off in the distance
from the men who had traveled
with him and his father.
It's an isolated story
about a kind of holiday,
a day set aside for silence
broken by Isaac's question,
posed uncertainly for his father:
Where is the lamb?
while from somewhere off in the distance,
they heard laughter of the men.

I imagine the boy could hear
the echo of his mother's last words
as they had left their home,
her wish that he not provoke
the men's malice. If a cold wind blew,

or the air was especially hot,
especially dry, Sarah would have given
additional warnings.

Imagine Sarah laughing with Isaac,
preparing him for a day with his father.
Imagine her in a wool or linen dress,
gathering courage for the madness she sensed,
the courage she would want to place
like a pebble inside her son
because she could not go on the journey.
She might have rubbed her hand
along his jawbone or behind his head
into the hollow of his neck;
or held his shoulders gently
for a minute; or maybe she didn't touch him.
Maybe she looked away from them all.
Later, Isaac would only have heard
his father's foolish lie.
Or have seen the way Abraham carried
the torch, the knife so carefully.
Or felt fear in his close grip.

Though I have no way of knowing,
these are fragments of the past I piece together.
They say before a murder the weather
may grow mild; that two men off in the distance
could laugh just when a miracle occurs.

Imagine Isaac's later version:
My father thought he heard God say
"sacrifice Isaac, your youngest son."
Imagine that he came to believe
in his father's hand halted above his face.

It's an isolated story.
Sometimes it makes me want to laugh.
Imagine Isaac hearing laughter and learning
each time that afternoon was recalled
to laugh a little at the telling and retelling.

Sculpted Royal Procession

They set up an imaginary ache,
these small tin men
(fifty-seven by thirty centimeters of them),
in a march that began in '39
across a wooden plate.
They carry baskets, a cylinder
that may contain silver, two open
umbrellas (one with a fluted edge)
and a king-bearing hammock,
swung from the tops of their heads
and held there by the raised hands
of three of the men (they may be
slaves to the tribe, or this
may mean honorable mention).
The bodies of all catch at the waist;
their legs spread like wishbones
to pigeon-toed feet
placed flat among the shadows
of their procession.
Their torsos are thin and bent
as though shaped and shaped again
by some pressure from above.
The baggage they carry day after day
becomes heavier with each motionless

step. I would be glad to find a key
beneath these tin men, a key
that would wind them forward.
Then they could lower their parcels,
place the king's hammock flat on the ground
where he would sit, his bronze crown shaken,
his large, square earring swaying to and fro.

The Giacomettis

Annette of the long neck
wears a knot of hair
above her bronze forehead.
Her shoulders are bound
by a ribbon drawn
down through her smock.

Without a word
from her lips,
I know she has always been proud
of her cheekbones
and holds her head still
to maintain those wide, shadowed planes.

Though both arms have vanished
for lack of occupation,
consider in her this constancy:
the stare toward nowhere
animating a blank wall.

■ ■

Falling Man
's elastic. Born in '51
he has come back

and back again
through the air
to the ground
though his foot never leaves the drum.

He swings and his hips
and his arms grow more graceful
each time his hammered metal
skill holds him back,
falling into,
rising out of,
an anvil of stillness.

■ ■

Put rouge beside the sideburns
of A Man in a Sweater
who belongs in the wind,
whose arms hang so heavily,
his brain will take flight.

A man in a sweater could be transformed
into a four-year-old
jumping from the corner

of a table in the nursery.
He says: *I used to be*
a woman, but now I'm a bird.

■ ■

Spoon Woman could bring a tune
from her bold-faced, parabolic
body. Take us
to town where they're dancing
'round a round summer totem.

Swollen with heat, feet stamp.
Hands are winding
to others, around
her dark, limbless concavity.

The smooth palm of her belly
shines with a will
for the deep, disembodied
laughter singing here
in this great hall
where we gawk.

■ ■

Woman (not posing) at twenty-one
stands ceremoniously out of line.

One breast is too low,
one knee's misshapen. I see
she imagines the sculptor
will be back. She hopes
he means her to be graceful.

She stands out of place
and the earth just turns.

Distance, Motion, and Sadness

A New Jersey transit train
speeds until everything close at hand
blurs. Only office parks and farms
far from the tracks seem clear.

Today we wind our clocks forward an hour.
Tomorrow I'll hear that your call came
fifty minutes after I left for the station.

At sixty miles an hour or so,
a second train glides into place beside this one.
Sometimes, watching the faces of other travelers
through two smeared windows
takes my breath away.

■ ■

People in New York City
move back several paces
when a train comes into the station.
That's because once in a while
someone insane
will push an innocent stranger
into the wheels of a train.

■ ■

I guess, she said, *to tell the truth. I guess,*
she said, *I guess he has left. I didn't think*
it would turn out this way. I know
there's a reason for everything, but to put it bluntly,
I thought he was here this time to stay.
I should think of something. I should try.
God, I'm too tired for this trip today.

■ ■

I never have gotten it clear
how time can erode a memory or wish.
Down on the pavement, a woman screamed,
Come back, you son of a bitch,
don't walk away from me.

Later I dreamed a man was calling me,
though he didn't hear my reply: *I'm here. I'm here.*

■ ■

Here's a story: Marconi
was in love with a woman
who lived in another nation.
Don't ask how he met her.
He wanted to talk to her all the time.
And that is how the telegraph was invented.

■ ■

There is a family beside a train—
two girls, two boys, a mother.
The father kisses each of them, the mother last.
He walks up metal steps
and turns to the left.
The whistle coos twice and the train
pulls out of the station.

■ ■

When a series of simple numbers told
the mean distance of each planet from the sun,
curvature of field had not been discovered or named.

■ ■

I remember my friend's father
with a camera tilted firmly
under his foul-weather hood in the rain
on a jetty in Nova Scotia.

By the time he was ready to snap the picture,
we were laughing so hard there were tears.

■ ■

Whenever a magnet is broken,
new poles occur
in each of the smaller magnets.

■ ■

We are on a train, in the twenty-third row
of the third car. The train is traveling
at forty-two miles an hour.
I ask if you'd like coffee in the bar.
I leave my book. You fold
the paper to save our seats.

The Hudson flows south to the left.
Between the cars, the wind blows so hard
I shut my eyes. You push with your shoulder
to force the door closed.

■ ■

Each part of nature
vibrates at a certain frequency
and that figure is a constant.

A digital record is discontinuous sound—
on and off, on and off—so fast

the human ear can't hear the silence,
the way moving pictures
are actually sequential stills
with invisible white space
between them.

■ ■

One night I dreamed of an older friend's failure
to see me among his children
though he had asked me to travel with them.

The next morning you boarded my bus to work
and walked silently down the aisle
past the empty seat beside me.

■ ■

Today it's a train out of the City.
You are reading the paper here beside me.

From time to time, you turn to tell me
something funny in the news.

Tomorrow you will be gone.
We do not talk of how we are
a small, mobile nation of love.

Strong Wind, Clear Window

Strong wind come, destroy our homes.

Paul Simon

1.

A young girl stands at the bathroom window,
watches the wind through white ruffled curtains,
sees a single leaf detach from an oak
in late summer. The first of the season.
It floats. It floats. It floats out of vision,
and *Julie, Julie,* her grandmother's name,
floats through her belly. She has a vision
of absence that's like a silk scarf settling.
The fact is that Julie is not alive.
How can the child turn from that clear window?

2.

Do you think watching the sun going down
about the bright green hills of this city
should help me understand how it is to go
alone, as we all go alone to die?
Maybe it is a little like sailing
into a pale but darkening sky,
or like a strangely detailed sad movie

that ends while the spectator sits in shock
at the last burning arrow and credits.
I've watched some go over that edge and not
come back. And I've wondered how that felt.

3.

My father died all of a sudden.
Walking away from his desk for a drink
of water, into the hall for some air,
out into the sunshine and toward his car,
he fell down and was cold dead in minutes.

I was too small to go to the funeral
where the minister said *the good die young*.
I still answered my father, *yes, sir*.

4.

The morning my mother died, I argued,
*How do you think you'll ever get better
if you won't get out of your bed and walk?*
She cried that I should leave her alone.

I did, then went home to find her bed empty.
They had already washed away the blood

that had choked her and poured out of her mouth.
Blood was my mother's final expression.
It left her like a hen leaving the farm
at dawn in a wild dog's hungry jaws.

5.

It's a winter of rotten news for many
of my friends. I think that I am in anguish
in the super store beside the apples.
A man I know comes up, inspects my groceries—
the pale, shiny faces against metal bars—
and my face for any signs of worry.
I think he sees them, little polished bulbs
of disturbance. I tell him I don't understand
why these things are happening. He puts
his big forehead down beside my small one
to whisper *nothing bad ever happens*.

I don't want to hear his version of love
or the grace that pushes my shopping cart
toward the soap. It seems to be precisely
nothing that happens while fears grow in us.
It is nothing, proclaimed as news or change
each minute and hour of each long day.

6.

I know an older man who's sturdy
but almost blind. Until a few months ago
he lived alone with a parrot he loved,
clipped the news for wisdom to send his sons
who are far away from home, and each day
for a few hours, he played his piano—
old tunes, *Star Dust, Melancholy Baby,*
Smoke Gets in Your Eyes.

Now his voice is gone.
He speaks through an electronic device,
writes one son he's *still a little tired.*
The surgeon says they will do anything
to help, because he's determined to live.
I think of his mechanical *hello,*
and I hope his will is the voice of God.

7.

To make it seem safer we tell ourselves lies.
I watch *Deer Hunter* and think of one shot—
guns, whiskey, drugs to ease us through the night.
I tell myself it's just a metaphor,

Nick coming back from death to blow his brains out.
I tell myself it's only a movie,
but slowly or fast, I'm frightened of dying.

8.

It's spring. I visit the lake by myself.
I go back to the rocks where we used to jump
and fall freely for thirty feet. Today
the water is high. On a rocky ledge,
I watch a spider scuttle back and forth
from my towel to the huge roots of a tree.

The sun catches us in its net of light,
and what I used to do while others watched,
I do alone. I take a few seconds
for courage and jump. Warmth rises along
my spine, something like freedom. I swim out
in the cold water. I swim out from shore
and then keep going. For just a minute,
the faces of all the leaves turn toward me.

A Litany of Trees

When I saw the bird, it frightened me,
flapping backward against the pavement
as though it would fly into the ground.

It was dying, I tell you, in the courtyard
of a bar where we are watching
leaves turn in the wind. You reach
across the table to take my hand.

But I am remembering walking with my father
when he saw a flying squirrel
lying dead against the sidewalk
like the small limb of a tree.

I believe he said something about dying
to make me stumble
into the shade of the tree.

You have amazing eyes, you say. *Hold my hand.*
But my arms lie still against my lap.
I am listening for the rain
that will fall through the leaves.
Around us, people gather their jackets and glasses.

Heading Home

After the climb, everything floats.
Leaving the mountains three days later,
I still feel in my spine
the way we went up step by step
and the tower started shaking
when two boys ran past us.

This girl on the bus
I took to be twelve
swears she's eighteen. Laughing, she shows me her license.
She's from Brooklyn; she's been on this bus for twenty-six hours.
She's wearing pink curlers; knows
a girl who stabbed her boyfriend
right through the sandy hair on his belly
because he'd been with another woman at Coney Island.
She says, *He must've been doing something good for her*
to make her go fool like that.
I ask, *Is that true?*

remembering the way from two hundred feet up
the edges of the mountains
lay as motionless
as the spars of large boats at anchor,
though, at the first platform,

they seemed to move
like old Mr. Levy years ago waving his arms
in the parking lot below my apartment.
Bending back, he yelled,
Jump! I'll catch you, then crept across the concrete
to his daughter's car. I felt like doing it.

The girl keeps laughing; she says, *They sell reefer in stores.*

I had to tell her about the time
Robert and I
stopped at the top of the double Ferris wheel
above the State Fair carnival
and my teeth started chattering. Robert grabbed the frame
and swung me until I cried,
Then he put his arm around my shoulders.
I want to say *All meanness is the same,*
but she's telling us her cousin
was shot in the head and left in an alley
because he wouldn't give up a pack of cigarettes.
She says, *I'd of give that guy my cigarettes.*
She's going to Fort Sill
where her boyfriend's stationed.
When he gets out in September, they're leaving Brooklyn.

At the last platform of the tower, I wanted to turn back
with only waist-high fence wires
and eighteen-wheel trucks carving paths
against the highway behind us
but the man climbing with me
said over and over *take your time*
until, at the top, the wind didn't matter.
We watched the blue mountains
still as a good prayer
and, on a far hill, a herd of cattle
like spiky metal jacks that had fallen into a decent pattern
just below our excited hands.

I ask, *Where will you live after Brooklyn?*

Rainstorm

The tulips have lost their heads,
the daffodils are battered.
The avenue resembles
a long field of picked cotton.
An old scarecrow shedding straw,
the sky drops rain down on us.
The windshield wipers pause, lift,
the way wishes rise through me
that it all will turn out right.

A flat green river delta
is where I spent my childhood,
watched my family's burials.
A highway skirts the iron fence
of the huge cemetery
where the graves I don't go to
are lost among the headstones
the way those first years recede
among too many terrors.

When I have fever, I still
want them back: mother, father . . .
Fever's just a kind of dream,
a road I go down to rest,

a shorter trip back home,
if home is where our loved ones'
corpses and ashes reside.
Their addresses stain the doors
of the dark, upright granites.

Most of the time, I stay well
in this far-away city
where the traffic moves faster
than a sudden change of weather.
There's lots of entertainment
in all the people's faces,
the curses they scream, the horns
of their cars answering life—
anger, greed, *make room for me*.

Say It's Quiet

I want you to understand
how the noise became a companion
I would never have dreamed
of shouting down.
Even the trees
seemed to drone.
The woman under bandages
and a newspaper blanket, though
just asleep on the pavement, might have
uttered the smeared words
of one half deaf, half mute.
And the traffic's song
was certain as the shuffle
of the wind in Kansas.

So, say it's always
New Year's Eve there and someone
is shouting the date
of the year just before
the silver ball
falls toward earth again.

Say it's darker
and quieter here. That at night by myself,

with only the hum
of the light of the moon,
I began to hear how quiet,
and walking by the cemetery, reciting
a few of the old, carved names, I raised
my hands a little and was pleased
to be alone. Then you'll know why,
when the pickup stopped and then
backed up and the man got out
and mumbled something, I called
him out of the shadows
and screamed, *Just get out of here*.

Quiet

My desk light shines
on a cream-colored box
painted with red roses.
I have taken out the photograph
I keep below one of the velvet-lined trays.
My father stands
looking out at a room of men
in the basement
of the First Methodist Church
where he taught
the Sunday Bible class.
He stands with right hand
in his trouser's pocket,
his jacket held back by his angled arm.
He could easily have taught
a snappy soft shoe.

If he turned from the lectern,
their careful eyes
would follow his walking.
I could never say
all that needs saying.
I am wastefully sorry
still for his dying.

This is nothing but a black-and-white photograph—
the quiet outline of an attentive room
with squares of gray linoleum,
six shiny doors,
a white-lettered announcement board.
The room is silent.
My past is silent.
I would like
to fold it all away
into something less.

Prayer for High Speeds

Rapid and Slow One, I begin
to say, Inventor of the spinning
sensations, don't let my body be taken
too quickly—fingers separated,
glass into bone, skin and blood
turned wrongsides, the sturdy
strings of my muscles
slung with mud in some ditch
beside a strip of asphalt.

You who have granted the one billion,
one hundred and forty million
seconds since my birth to this colorful sphere,
let me be cast out to the black-eyed stars
miles from earth's old fee
for salt and water slowly. Seal
the speeds I move at with safety.

When wheels spin hot on the tar,
wash a cool spill of grace over the asphalt.
Unravel the lace of life slowly from me.
Let me drift, not speed, into eternity.

I Sleep Now

Returned from a party
and the woebegone logic
of a lecture on the lover
I should have,
I am greeted by the circle
of bright-faced books
piled around my pillow.
Go to sleep I say to the books.
But they have needs.

I hold one briefly
while my eyes close
at some space between the lines.
It moves down my shoulder
to the crook of a weary arm.
All night, we slip together and apart.
Their small spines edge
to the corners of my quilt.
I may, dreaming, knock one out of bed.
This doesn't disturb the rest of a book.

Closed under its assured title,
its personalities are fixed as words,
sometimes seductive, sometimes dismal

but books, oh books, my very busy books
usually keep a proper distance
and are almost always faithful.